KUNG FU

NEIL MORRIS

HEINEMANN LIBRARY
CHICAGO, ILLINOIS

© 2001 Reed Educational & Professional Publishing
Published by Heinemann Library,
an imprint of Reed Educational & Professional Publishing,
Chicago, Illinois

Customer Service 888-454-2279

Visit our website at www.heinemannlibrary.com

Designed by Ken Vail Graphic Design, Cambridge
Illustrations by Simon Girling & Associates (Mike Lacey)
Originated by Dot Gradations
Printed by Wing King Tong in Hong Kong

05 04 03 02 01
10 9 8 7 6 5 4 3 2 1

Library of Congress Cataloging-in-Publication Data
Morris, Neil, 1946-
  Kung fu / Neil Morris.
      p. cm. -- (Get going! Martial arts)
Includes bibliographical references (p.) and index.
  ISBN 1-58810-040-5
  1. Kung fu--Juvenile literature. [1. Kung fu.] I. Title.
  GV1114.7 .M67 2001
  796.815'9--dc21
                            00-013256

Acknowledgments
The Publishers would like to thank the following for permission to reproduce photographs:
Corbis, p. 12; Simon T. Lailey p. 7 bottom; Rex Features, p. 7 top; Rex Features/Kuan Cheng/Xinhua, p. 5; Ronald Grant Archive, p. 29; All other photographs by Trevor Clifford.

Cover photograph reproduced with permission of Earl and Nazima Kowall/Corbis.

Every effort has been made to contact copyright holders of any material reproduced in this book. Any omissions will be rectified in subsequent printings if notice is given to the Publisher.

The Publisher would like to thank Sifu Kevin Loftus for helping us improve the accuracy of this text.

Some words are shown in bold, **like this.** You can find out what they mean by looking in the glossary.

Chinese words are shown in italics, *like this.* You can find out what they mean by looking at the chart on page 30.

CONTENTS

! Please remember that martial arts need to be taught by a qualified, registered teacher. Do not try any of the techniques and movements in this book without such an instructor present.

WHAT IS KUNG FU?

Kung fu is a general term used for all Chinese martial arts. Since the People's Republic of China has a greater population than any other country in the world—at least 1.2 billion people, or about a fifth of the world's population—it is not surprising that there are hundreds of different forms of kung fu. The term *kung fu* is not easy to translate, but the closest equivalent is "skill over time." The Chinese word for "martial art" is *wushu,* a term that is sometimes also used to cover all the different Chinese arts, in a similar way to kung fu. Some people use the term *kung fu* to refer to the exercise and self-defense aspects of the martial art, and use *wushu* to refer to the competitive sport.

All over the country, there are kung fu clubs with experienced teachers.

NORTHERN FOOT, SOUTHERN FIST

The many different schools of kung fu are traditionally divided into styles that came originally from northern and southern China. There is a phrase "northern foot, southern fist," which means that the northern styles contain a lot of kicking techniques, whereas the southern styles are based more on use of the hands. Northern styles have a great deal of movement, and may have developed their leg techniques in ancient times when many opponents were mounted horsemen. Southern styles include more close-quarter techniques, and some are so specialized that they are still named after the family names of their founders, such as *hung gar, lau gar,* and *mok gar.* In Chinese, g*ar* means "family."

WHERE TO LEARN AND PRACTICE

This book tells you how to get started in kung fu. It also shows and explains some kung fu techniques, so that you can understand and practice them. But you must always remember that you cannot learn any martial art just from a book. To be a serious student of kung fu, you must go to regular lessons with a qualified teacher, so that you learn all the techniques properly and then repeat and practice them many times.

YOUR KUNG FU CLUB

Choose your club carefully. It should have an experienced teacher and it should be part of a martial arts association. The list on page 31 gives the names and addresses of organizations that can give you national and local information, as well as lists of clubs.

These students are giving an outdoor demonstration of kung fu.

KUNG FU THROUGH HISTORY

All the world's martial arts can be traced back to Ancient China, which had a strong influence on Korea, Japan, and the rest of the Far East. Chinese clans, families, and individuals learned to defend themselves during many troubled periods in ancient times. About 2,500 years ago, there were battles between huge armies with horse-drawn chariots, bronze swords, and deadly crossbows. The Chinese armies had a total of more than six million soldiers, and in one battle in 260 B.C.E., half a million men were killed. The land was also full of bandits, which encouraged young men to learn to defend themselves and their families.

This map shows Korea, Japan, and China.

About 1,500 years ago, a famous monastery and temple were founded in the mountains of Henan province in central China. In order to protect their temple—called Shaolin—against bandits, the monks trained hard to become fit and strong. Around 520 C.E., an Indian monk called Bodhidharma came to the Shaolin Temple. He taught a form of **meditation** known as **Zen Buddhism**, or *Chan* in Chinese. The Shaolin Temple became a leading martial arts school, combining self-defense skills with a peaceful way of life.

Over 1,000 years later, a fire destroyed the temple. Some say it was started by a monk on behalf of the emperor, who feared the influence of the temple. According to legend, just four monks and a nun survived the fire, and they became the founders of modern martial arts.

These life-sized warrior figures were buried in 210 B.C.E. near the tomb of the Chinese Emperor.

WING CHUN

The nun who survived the Shaolin fire, Ng Mui, had learned martial arts at the temple. Moving to the south of China, she met a young woman named Yim Wing Chun, whom she taught. Ng Mui taught her a new form of kung fu that would allow a smaller person to defend herself using skill and speed, not strength. Wing Chun, whose name means "radiant springtime," was being bothered by a bully who wanted to marry her. Her father told the bully that his daughter would only marry someone who could beat her in a fight. Wing Chun easily defended herself against the bully and the rest of his gang, which left her free to marry the young man she loved. Today, the style of kung fu that Ng Mui developed, known as *wing chun,* is one of the best known throughout the world. Many of the techniques in this book are based on *wing chun.*

This is a Shaolin temple in China today.

IN THE KWOON

Kung fu is practiced and performed in a casual training outfit, which is traditionally black. It is best to buy a suit through your club, but you do not need one right away. For the first few sessions, a sweatshirt and sweatpants or a T-shirt and jogging pants will probably do, but check this with the club first. When you do buy your kung fu suit, make sure that it is large enough so that your movements will not be restricted in any way.

It is important to take good care of your outfit. Keep it clean, wash and iron it regularly, and fold it carefully after each training session. A neat and tidy appearance shows that you have the right attitude toward training. Inside the training hall, called a *kwoon,* you should wear special, lightweight kung fu shoes. For the first few sessions, tennis shoes will do.

Most kung fu suits are black.

 SAFETY

In order not to harm yourself or anyone else, do not wear a watch or any jewelry. Keep your fingernails and toenails trimmed short. Pull long hair back, but do not use metal clips.

Make sure that you are in good shape for active exercise, and do not train if you are ill. Exercise should not hurt, so never push yourself to a point at which you feel pain.

It is a good idea for boys to wear a protective cup. Both boys and girls should wear mouthguards in any form of competition.

Any martial art can be dangerous if it is not performed properly. Never fool around inside or outside the training hall—or at home or in school—by showing off or pretending to have a real fight.

COURTESY

It is important for martial arts students to show respect to everyone and everything to do with their sport. As a sign of respect, there are several formal kung fu greetings. They vary in different schools. This is a *wing chun* greeting.

1 Stand with your feet together and your arms at your sides.

2 Make a fist with one hand and place it in the palm of your other hand, in front of you at chin level. Make sure that your face is friendly and not **aggressive.**

WOODEN DUMMY

Some kung fu schools use a wooden dummy that is designed to be an imitation of the human body. Kung fu artists use it to practice and develop their striking and blocking techniques.

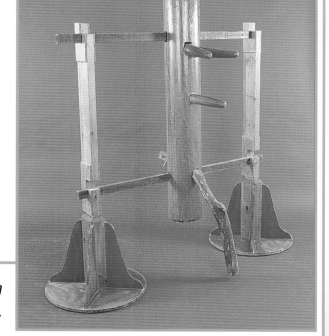

The Chinese name for the training dummy is mook yan jong.

WARMING UP

Kung fu involves a lot of very physical exercise. It is important to warm your body up and stretch your muscles before training, so that you do not injure yourself. At your club, you will always start your sessions with some warm-up exercises. You might begin by walking or jogging in place for a couple of minutes and then go on to do some stretching exercises.

IMPORTANT

- Drink a lot of water, and do not exercise too hard when it is very hot or humid.

- Do not exercise when you are ill or injured.

- Try not to breathe too hard and fast when you are exercising or resting.

- Do not hold your breath while you are exercising.

- When you are stretching, you should always remain comfortable and your muscles should not hurt. If you feel pain, stop at once.

- Begin your exercise immediately after warming up. You should do some cool-down activities immediately after exercising.

ARM CIRCLES

1 Stand up straight with your feet a shoulder-width apart.

2 Stretch your arms out to the sides at shoulder level and then rotate them in forward circles. Do ten circles, making the circles as large as you can.

3 Repeat the ten circles, this time backwards.

UPPER BACK STRETCH

1 Stand up straight and clasp your hands together behind your back, locking your fingers together.

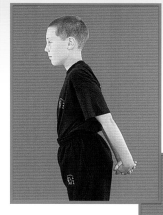

2 Lift your hands up as high as you can and as far away from your back as possible. Hold this position for a count of five, then return to the starting position.

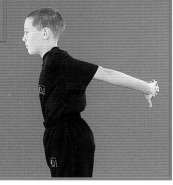

3 Repeat the exercise five times.

QUADRICEPS STRETCH

Your quadriceps are the large muscles at the front of your thighs.

1 Stand up straight, with your feet a shoulder-width apart.

2 Raise your left knee and take hold of your left ankle with your left hand.

3 Take your left leg back until your heel is close to your buttock.

4 Hold this position for a count of ten, keeping your knees close together.

5 Repeat the exercise with the other leg.

See page 25 for cooling down exercises.

11

STYLES AND FORMS

ANIMAL MOVEMENTS

Many of the hundreds of different kung fu styles developed in ancient times from people carefully watching and copying the movements of animals. The tiger, leopard, dragon, crane, and snake are the most famous animal styles. The tiger and leopard styles use slashing strikes, developed from the strong claws of the big wild cats. The dragon style is also a very powerful style.

Crane-style kung fu came from copying the bird's movements.

The crane and the snake are less **aggressive** styles, and are the basis for much of the famous *wing chun* style of kung fu. Many of the techniques in this book are based on *wing chun*.

The crane is a tall bird with long legs that appears in many Chinese legends. In the crane style, the martial artist makes her thumb and fingers into a beak shape. She pecks at her opponent with her two hand-beaks.

A popular style of kung fu is the crane style.

The "snake" usually coils up and then suddenly springs at her opponent, striking with her fingertips.

Another style follows snake movements.

PATTERNS

Kung fu styles have their own forms, or **patterns.** These are made up of a series of set moves that are practiced to improve technique and help an artist learn about attack, defense, and **counter-attack.** The moves are like training drills with an imaginary opponent. As you learn the forms, your instructor, or *sifu* in Chinese, will constantly check to make sure your technique is correct.

The patterns all start from a basic training position. To get in position, make relaxed fists and pull them up to the sides of your chest. Place your legs a shoulder-width apart, and bend your knees slightly.

This is the basic training position.

This student models the opening hand.

HAND POSITIONS

In the *wing chun* style, several basic hand positions are used and practiced throughout the forms. As you practice, these hand positions help make the wrists stronger and more flexible.

To make the opening hand, called *tan sau* in Chinese, open your left hand and very slowly move it forward until your elbow is in front of your chest. Your right hand should be in the middle of your body.

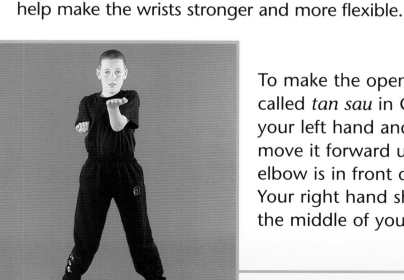

The opening hand is a basic hand position.

PUNCHING

Kung fu punches are famous for being very powerful. The *wing chun* basic punch, in particular, develops a lot of power, even though it often travels a very short distance. You can practice punching without an opponent. When you have learned the basic skills, you may be allowed to practice against an opponent who is holding a **focus pad.**

The power of the punch comes at the very last moment, so a powerful blow can be made over just an inch, or a few centimeters. You must learn to focus all of your energy at the right moment, or the energy will be wasted.

WING CHUN PUNCH

1 Start from the basic training position, shown on page 13. Open one hand as you put it forward and point your fingers at the imaginary target.

2 As you start to make a punch by straightening your elbow, close your fingers to make a fist. Put your thumb on top of your fist as you clench your fingers tightly.

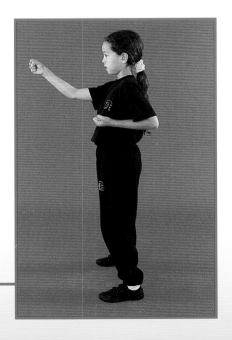

3 Hit the target with your lower three knuckles, focusing all your energy into your fist, and keeping your thumb on top. Be sure that your arm stays slightly bent when you punch, so as not to put too much strain on your elbow.

There is a special version of this move called the one-inch punch, *chun ging.* It is very short and extremely powerful.

THE CENTER LINE

Many kung fu punches are aimed at the center of the opponent's body. The punches are aimed based on an imaginary center line running from the top of the head down the middle of the face and body.

From this center line, you can divide the body into **zones** and **gates.** There are three basic zones. The high zone goes from the top of the head to the chest. The middle zone goes from the pit of the stomach to the groin. The low zone goes from the hips to the toes. Each of these zones has an inner and an outer gate, which lie on either side of the center line.

In *wing chun* kung fu, students are trained to use the right block and **counter-attack,** depending on which zone is being attacked. At the same time, the student will try to open up the opponent's center line with the blocks.

STRIKING

Strikes are like punches, but they use other parts of the hand and arm instead of the closed fist. They are practiced without an opponent or as part of a training drill. Later you may be allowed to try some of the moves in **sparring** sessions with a partner, which give you the opportunity to test the skills you have learned and practiced. At first, all the sparring will be prearranged. This means that both partners agree beforehand what they are going to do. This makes it easier for both partners to learn how to use combinations properly and get their timing right.

THRUSTING FINGERS

This powerful strike comes originally from the snake style of kung fu and uses strong fingers to attack an opponent's eyes. As in the basic punch, all the striker's energy should be put into his or her fingers at the very last moment.

 SPARRING SAFETY

When sparring or just practicing a strike, you must concentrate very hard and make sure that you do not actually hit your partner. The balance you learned during all the hours of practice without a partner will help you. Always work with your partner, so that you help each other and learn together.

KNIFE HAND

The knife hand is similar to the "**karate chop**" that a lot of people associate with karate. In this strike, the target is hit with the little-finger edge of the hand.

PALM-HEEL STRIKE

This sort of strike is particularly useful if your opponent is moving forward, so that he or she walks into it and increases its force. It is most effective when aimed at the chin or jaw.

ELBOW STRIKE

This is a powerful short-range strike that thrusts the point of the elbow into the opponent's jaw, chin, or ribs. In this case, the student has also taken the opportunity to grab his opponent's wrist. This particular move, called the grabbing hand, or *lap sau*, is used often in kung fu. It helps you keep your opponent where you want him or her to be.

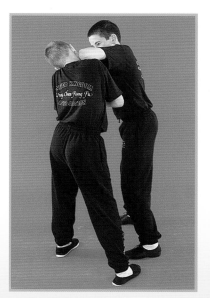

KICKING

Kung fu kicks are powerful weapons. They have a greater reach than punches or other strikes, but because they have to travel a long way to hit their target, an opponent has more time to avoid them. Most kung fu kicks begin with the leg bent at the knee. The leg is then straightened to hit the target with the foot, but never with the toes. It is important to keep the leg slightly bent, so as not to put too much strain on the knee.

The northern Chinese kung fu styles have high, spectacular kicks. In the southern styles, such as *wing chun,* the kicks are lower and tend to be aimed at the opponent's ankles, shins, or knees.

FRONT KICK

You will probably learn this kick first, since it is the most basic kicking technique. From the basic training position, bend your knees and keep your right fist up to guard your face. Bring your left leg forward and raise your left foot, pulling the toes back.

When your left knee is high, thrust out your left leg, pushing your hips into the kick. Imagine that you are hitting the target, your opponent's stomach, with your heel. Remember to keep your guard up during the kick.

SIDE KICK

For this kick, approach your opponent from a sideways position. This beginning position is often called a cat **stance.** Raise your right foot and drive your heel downward. In a real situation, this would hit your opponent's knee.

HOOK KICK

This self-defense technique is a basic move in the form of kung fu developed by martial arts expert and movie star Bruce Lee. It is unusual because you do not lift your knee, you just give a circular kick straight from the hip.

BLOCKING

In any martial art, players have to learn to defend themselves against attacks by their opponent. Even the best attacking martial artists also need good defending techniques. Many of the basic moves in kung fu start with a block, used to fend off an attack by the opponent. This acts as a good reminder that the true spirit of all martial arts is never to strike the first blow but to defend against **aggression.** A good block will upset the opponent's balance and force them into a position in which they are open to a **counter-attack.**

 SAFETY FIRST

Remember that you must only practice blocking moves at your martial arts club, where they will be properly supervised. If you are pretending to hit your opponent, aim to fall well short of your target. Every martial artist must be responsible for the safety of his or her partner as well as him- or herself.

Two basic blocks use either side of the blocking arm to turn an opponent's punch away from or across the body.

FIRST BLOCK

As the opponent comes in with a punch, raise your right hand with the palm side up. Block your opponent's punch with the thumb side of your hand and arm. This will divert the strike across your opponent's body so that he or she cannot reach you with either fist.

SECOND BLOCK

1 This time, as your opponent comes in with a punch, you again raise your right hand. Your hand should be palm side up.

2 Now block your opponent's punch with the little finger side of your hand and arm. This diverts his or her strike across your body. You can even take the opportunity to turn the blocking hand into a fist and punch your opponent.

RELAXATION AND ENERGY

Chinese martial artists strongly believe in relaxing both the mind and the body. One way to do this is by breathing correctly. Instead of just using the upper part of the chest to breathe, use the lower chest and diaphragm—the large sheet of muscle below the lungs that plays an important part in our breathing. Good breathing helps relaxation, and Chinese martial artists believe that this produces *qi*, or energy. They believe that *qi* is stored in an area called the *dantien*, a spot just below the navel that is the body's center of gravity.

STICKING HANDS

Much of kung fu involves close-range **sparring** between two partners. This means that attacks can come very quickly, one after another. Martial artists have to learn to recognize the moves that are coming and deal with them correctly and quickly.

Sticking hands, or *chi sau*, is a special form of training for close combat that is unique to kung fu. It teaches you how to deal with all the pushing, grabbing, and wrestling that go on. You practice getting in close to your partner, blocking his or her moves and **counter-attacking** with your own.

In order to develop the skills of sticking hands, you need to go to regular kung fu classes and learn from a good teacher. You work in pairs, and both partners can learn the basics of close fighting skills without hurting each other. Beginners start with single sticking hands and eventually move on to the double form of training.

These starting sequences give an idea of the two forms.

SINGLE HAND

1 The boy on the right makes the opening hand we saw earlier, which is also a palm-up block. The boy on the left rests his wrist on his opponent's arm in a resting hand position.

2 The boy on the right attacks with a palm strike, which the other boy blocks by forcing it down with a "sinking hand."

3 The boy on the left turns the block into an attack by punching toward his opponent. The other boy uses a wing-arm block by raising his right arm, but keeping his wrist relaxed.

4 The two partners return to the first position and go through the sequence again and again.

DOUBLE HANDS

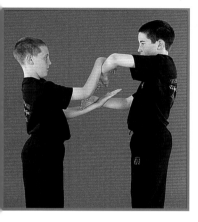

1 The boy on the right rests his right arm on the outside of his opponent's arm. The other boy has his right arm on the outside of his opponent's arm.

2 Both partners roll their hands up and down, changing their hand positions, but constantly keeping in contact. When you get used to this, you will start to feel what your partner is going to do next.

3 The boy on the right pushes his right arm to the outside of the other boy's arm. This is called changing **gates.**

4 Now, the boy on the right pushes his left arm through, grabs the other boy's neck gently, and pulls his head forward. He is now in control, because the other boy's arms are trapped.

5 For practice, this sequence could be done in different ways, and then be repeated.

SELF-DEFENSE

Many people take up a martial art to learn self-defense. They want to learn techniques that will be useful in the event that they are unfortunate enough to need them. The various schools of kung fu all have different approaches to self-defense, but most of their moves lend themselves naturally to this use.

Learning kung fu skills builds up your self-confidence, especially if you are shy by nature. Others will see that you are confident—that is, happy with yourself without being a show-off—and you are less likely to be seen as a target by any potential bully. Many kung fu moves are based on using a small amount of energy to defeat much greater force. This means that a small, calm person can overcome a larger, more **aggressive** opponent.

FOCUS PADS

Remember, when you punch in a **sparring** session, your fist must fall just short of your opponent so that he or she is not actually touched. You may wear special fist mitts in case you accidentally do strike your opponent. You can practice punching by having a partner hold up one or two **focus pads.** Punching against pads will give you confidence to hit hard. The pads can also be used for practicing kicks and other strikes.

PROFESSIONAL PRACTICE

Kung fu can be an excellent way to defend yourself. But remember, you must only practice self-defense moves with your instructor present, so that you see the correct way to do them. As with any martial art move, learning the timing is very important.

Using any martial art in self-defense is a last resort. If someone is bothering you, it is always best to tell them that you do not want a fight. If possible, find help as quickly as you can. Tell a teacher, your parents, or any grown-up you trust. Always avoid a fight, but never keep problems to yourself.

COOLING DOWN

It is important to cool down gently after high-energy exercise such as kung fu. You can do this by jogging, walking, deep breathing, and doing some stretching exercises. These could be the same exercises you did to warm up, shown on pages 10–11.

Or you could do some other stretches. For example, windmills are similar to arm circles, except that you swing one arm at a time. Some students like to cool down by doing some **patterns** to music.

Do arm circles to cool down after exercising.

Gently stretch your back.

It is also good to do a quadriceps stretch.

TAI CHI

If you have heard of tai chi, you probably think of it as a system of Chinese exercises. It is true that in the parks and open spaces of modern China, especially early in the morning, you see people going through tai chi movements. Many tai chi students are older, retired people. These routines are very good for their health.

Tai chi chuan, to use the full name, is in fact a martial art. It is a form of kung fu, and its name means "great ultimate boxing." According to tradition, it was first developed by a thirteenth-century priest named Chang San Feng, who studied at the Shaolin Temple. He was a **Taoist** who was supposedly influenced in his development of the art by watching the fluid movements of a snake and a stork as they fought. Tai chi is still strongly linked to Taoist beliefs.

THE SINGLE WHIP

This example of a tai chi movement and position is known as *tan pien,* or the "single whip."

1 Put your left leg forward and put your weight on it. Hold your left hand in front of you. Hold your right hand behind you, curling your fingers and thumb into a hook position.

2 Slowly and smoothly turn your right foot outward and begin to move your weight onto the back foot. At the same time, begin to lower your left hand. This is actually a block against a striking technique.

3 Bend your right leg until it forms a right angle. Slide your left arm down your left leg, keeping your back straight. Throughout the exercise, keep your eyes looking forward at an imaginary opponent.

YIN AND YANG

Many Chinese martial arts are linked to religious or **philosophical** beliefs. Some are related to the Taoist beliefs of yin and yang. Taoists follow the teachings of Lao-tzu, who lived in the sixth century B.C.E. and believed that people should live simple lives in tune with nature. In the symbol of yin and yang, the dark and the light are clasped together, and each contains a tiny amount of the other. The yin represents the dark, cool, and soft. The yang represents the light, hot, and hard. Some kung fu schools are said to be "hard," while others are "soft."

ALL AROUND THE WORLD

Kung fu has grown and spread from China throughout the world. At the same time, it has kept its many different schools and approaches, which makes it complicated as a world sport. The International Wushu Federation, based in Beijing, China, organizes world championships that have six different events. There are separate sections for men and women. Many of the events use traditional Chinese weapons. The events include a northern style with jumps and footwork, and a southern style with hand movements, tai chi, and fighting with a **broadsword, cudgel,** and spear.

GRADING

Unlike Japanese and Korean martial arts, kung fu does not have an official form of grading to show students how they are progressing. However, some schools use a series of colored sashes, such as this:

sash color		*grade*
yellow	≈	1st (beginner)
orange	≈	2nd
green	≈	3rd
blue	≈	4th
brown	≈	5th
black	≈	10th degree (expert)

BRUCE LEE

Many people around the world would never have heard of kung fu if it had not been for Bruce Lee. Born Lee Yuan Kam in San Francisco in 1940, Bruce spent most of his childhood in Hong Kong, where he learned kung fu. Then he studied **philosophy** at the University of Washington. During the 1960s, he started acting on television. His big break came in 1971, when he returned to Hong Kong to make a martial arts film called *Fists of Fury*. In 1973, he made *Enter the Dragon,* which is considered the best kung fu movie of all time.

Ip Man, a **grand master** in *wing chun,* was Bruce Lee's kung fu teacher. Lee later developed his own form of kung fu, called *jeet kune do,* "the way of the intercepting fist," or JKD. He always insisted that this was not a new style, but a way to free martial artists from clinging to specific styles or methods. He wrote two books, *Tao of Jeet Kune Do,* and *Chinese Gung Fu: The Philosophical Art of Self-Defense,* that explain his ideas about the martial arts.

Bruce Lee's films, which are full of action and amazing fight sequences, were very popular in the 1970s. They increased the world's awareness of kung fu, **karate,** and the martial arts in general.

Bruce Lee starred in the action film Enter the Dragon.

CHINESE WORDS

Chinese word	Meaning	Chinese word	Meaning
chi sau	sticking hands	mook yan jong	training dummy
chun ging	one-inch punch	qi	energy
dantien	spot just below the navel, the body's center of gravity	sifu	instructor
		tai chi chuan	"great ultimate boxing," a martial art
gar	family	tan pien	single whip
jeet kune do	"way of intercepting a fist," a form of kung fu developed by Bruce Lee	tan sau	opening hand position
		wing chun	style of kung fu, meaning "radiant springtime"
kwoon	training hall		
lap sau	grabbing hand move	wushu	martial art

GLOSSARY

aggressive — forceful or hostile. The use of hostile behavior is aggression.

broadsword — sword with a wide blade

counter-attack — attack that replies to an attack by an opponent

cudgel — short club used as a weapon

focus pad — pad or padded glove that can be held up by a partner so that the opponent can practice punching and kicking against it

gate — area of attack and defense that covers certain parts of the body

grand master — expert of the highest class

karate — Japanese martial art that uses hands and feet to make high-energy punches, strikes, and kicks

meditation — exercising the mind by thinking, especially about religion

pattern — set of moves learned as a training drill

philosophy — set of beliefs, often designed to help people be good or become wise. These beliefs are described as philosophical.

sparring — practice contest between two martial arts students, sometimes with the moves agreed upon in advance

stance — position of the body, with the feet in a special place and the arms held in a special way

Taoist — following the philosophy of Lao-tzu, who lived in ancient China in the sixth century B.C.E.

Zen Buddhism — form of the Buddhist religion in which meditation is particularly important

zone — area of attack and defense that covers certain parts of the body

MORE BOOKS TO READ

Blackall, Bernie. *Martial Arts*. Chicago: Heinemann Library, 1998.

Casey, Kevin. *Kung Fu*. Vero Beach, Fla.: Rourke Corporation, 1994.

Knotts, Bob. *Martial Arts*. Danbury, Conn.: Children's Press, 2000.

Randall, Pamela. *Kung Fu*. New York: Rosen Publishing Group, Inc., 1999.

TAKING IT FURTHER

American Chinese Martial Arts Federation
North American Headquarters—Kung Fu U.S.A.
15930 Halliburton Road
Hacienda Height, CA 97145
Telephone: (626) 318-8718

Chinese Kung-Fu Wu-Su Association
28 West 27th Street
New York, NY 10001
Telephone: (212) 725-0535

Chong's Wing Chun Kung Fu Association
7039 S. Land Park Drive
Sacramento, CA 95831
Telephone: (916) 424-4710

Evolving Body Mind (EBM) Kung Fu Association
666 63rd Street
Oakland, CA 94609
Telephone: (510) 658-3378

Fong's Wing Chun Gung Fu Federation
920 South Craycroft Road
Tucson, AZ
Telephone: (520) 747-9553

INDEX